African

ART & CULTURE

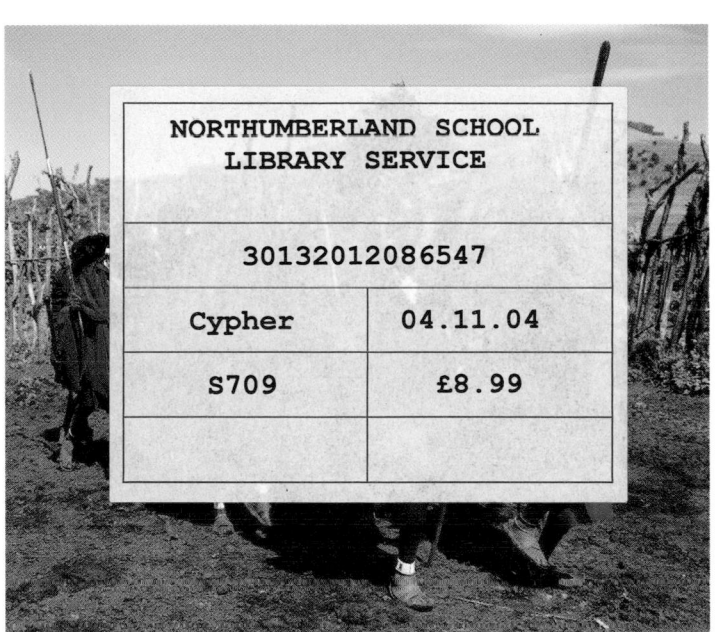

Jane Bingham

Raintree

www.raintreepublishers.co.uk
Visit our website to find out more information about **Raintree** books.

To order:

 Phone 44 (0)1865 888113

 Send a fax to 44 (0)1865 314091

Visit the Raintree bookshop at **www.raintreepublishers.co.uk** to browse our catalogue and order online.

First published in Great Britain by Raintree, Halley Court, Jordan Hill, Oxford OX2 8EJ, part of Harcourt Education.
Raintree is a registered trademark of Harcourt Education Ltd.

© Harcourt Education Ltd 2003
First published in paperback in 2004.
The moral right of the proprietor has been asserted.

Editorial: Nancy Dickmann and Louise Galpine
Design: Ron Kamen and Paul Davies and Associates
Illustrations: Nicholas Beresford-Davies and Paul Davies
Picture Research: Peter Morris and Maria Joannou
Production: Séverine Ribierre

Originated by Dot Gradations
Printed and bound in China by South China Printing Company

ISBN 184421044 8 (hardback)   ISBN 1844210499 (paperback)
07 06 05 04 03   08 07 06 05 04
10 9 8 7 6 5 4 3 2 1   10 9 8 7 6 5 4 3 2 1

British Library Cataloguing in Publication Data
Bingham, Jane
    World Art and Culture: African
    709.6
A full catalogue record for this book is available from the British Library.

Acknowledgements
The publishers would like to thank the following for permission to reproduce photographs: Alamy pp.**14** (Gary Cook), **31** (Robert Harding Picture Library); Art Archive pp.**9** (Antenna Gallery Dakar Senegal/ Dagli Orti), **50** (Museum of Modern Art New York/ Album/ Joseph Martin); Corbis pp.**11** (Anthony Bannister), **32** (Bowers Museum), **15** (Brian Vikander), **36** (Burstein Collection), **25** (Charles and Josette Lenares), **27** (Charles O'Rear), **49** (Contemporary African Art Collection), **26**, **33** (Dave Houser), **41** (Diego Lezama Orezzoli), **13**, **45** (Images of Africa), **16** (Lindsay Hebberd), **21** (Margaret Courtney-Clarke), **5** (Nik Wheeler), **35** (North Carolina Museum of Art), **29** (Otto Lang), **30** (Owen Franklin), **43** (Peter Johnson), **51** (Philadelphia Museum of Art), **10** (Pierre Colombel), **48** (Seattle Art Museum) **19** (Werner Forman), **23** (Yann Arthurs-Bertrand); Panos pictures pp.**37**, **39**; Panos pictures p.**42** (Liba Taylor); Peter Evans p.**12**; Werner Forman Archive pp.**7**, **8**, **38**, **40** (British Museum), **46** (Musée Royal de l'Afrique Centrale/Tervuren), **18** (National Museum, Lagos), **44** (Susan Vogel Collection, New York).

Cover photographs of a wooden portrait of the head of an Ife king reproduced with permission of Corbis/Kimbell Art Museum, and of the Chief of Bonwire's grandson wearing a 50-year-old Kente cloth robe reproduced with permission of Corbis/Margaret Courtney-Clarke.

The publishers would like to thank Dr Tavy Aherne for her assistance in the preparation of this book.

Contents

Words printed in the text in bold, **like this**, are explained in the Glossary.

Introduction

The continent of Africa takes up more than a fifth of the Earth's surface. It is a land of dramatically contrasting climates. Stretching across most of northern Africa is the vast Sahara desert, while the Kalahari and Namib deserts cover large areas of southern Africa. In the centre of the continent, around the equator, are steamy tropical forests. On either side of the rainforests lie hot, dry grasslands, known as **savannah**. Closer to the coasts, where the weather is cooler, there are woodlands and mountains.

Different peoples

More than 1000 languages are spoken in Africa, and there are many different ways of life across the continent. The majority of Africans are farmers, living in villages on the vast grasslands, while some have a wandering life as cattle herders. Other people live as **nomads**, travelling through the deserts, and setting up tents wherever they stop, and a small number are hunters and gatherers of food, deep within the rainforests. Many Africans today live and work in towns and cities, but they often keep strong links with their villages in the countryside.

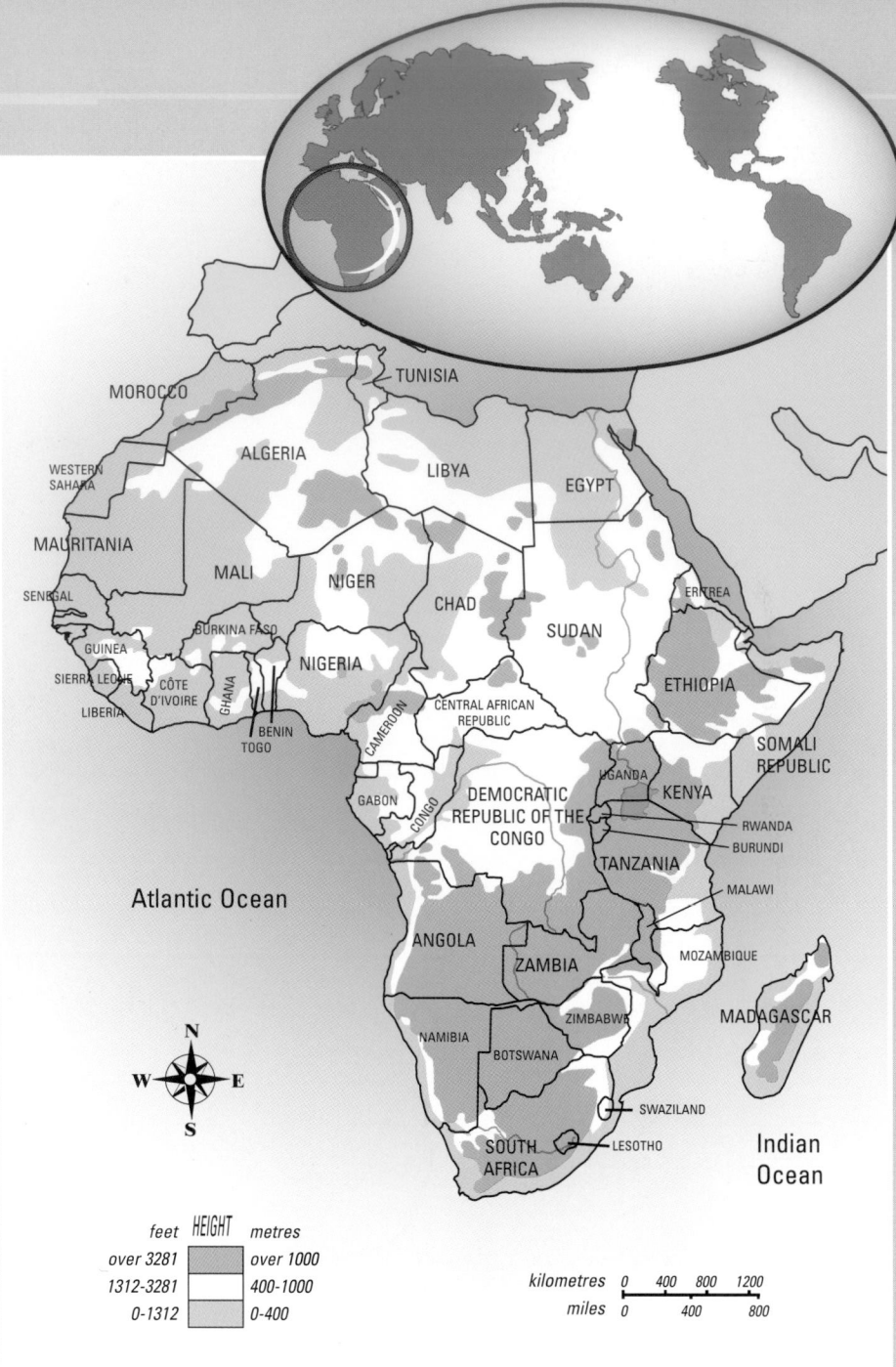

This map shows the vast extent of the continent of Africa, home to many different cultures and languages.

Different art

The type of art that people produce depends on where they live in Africa. People from the southern edge of West Africa live near the rainforests, and have developed strong traditions of woodcarving. West Africa is also rich in iron and gold, so fine

Art is everywhere in Africa. Here, men and women, dressed in brilliantly coloured, patterned clothes, have set up an open-air market beside the city walls of Djenne in West Africa.

metalwork is produced here. In contrast to the settled people of the rainforests and the grassland farmers, the herders of the grasslands and **sahel** areas make artworks that are easily portable, such as baskets and head stools. The wandering people of the desert, who travel very lightly, concentrate on the arts of the body, such as body painting and jewellery making.

Types of art

Art is everywhere in African life, from the pots and baskets used for cooking and storing food, to the hand-woven clothes and jewellery still worn by people in traditional communities. African homes are often decorated inside and out, sculptures and masks are used in religious ceremonies, and the streets of African towns and cities are lined with colourful hand-painted signs and advertisements.

This book covers different aspects of African art – such as pottery, textiles and metalwork – and concentrates on individual works within these groupings. By looking at examples from many parts of Africa, it aims to build up a picture of the richness and variety of African art.

The history of Africa

Africa has a very long history – experts believe that all human life began there around 5 million years ago. Little is known about prehistoric life in Africa but rock paintings survive from around 25,000 BCE, showing people hunting wild animals. By 7500 BCE people in Africa were making pots, and around 1000 years later, they began to keep cattle. At this time, the area that is now the Sahara desert was covered by grassland.

Early kingdoms

Around 5000 BCE, the weather in Africa became much warmer. Gradually, the grasslands of northern Africa dried up and the Sahara desert was formed. From this time on, the Sahara formed a barrier between northern and southern Africa, and the two halves of the country developed in very different ways.

Although most of northern Africa was covered by desert, the land beside the River Nile was very fertile and good for farming. From about 3000 BCE, a series of powerful kingdoms grew up around the Nile. The first and most successful of these was the kingdom of ancient Egypt.

Around 1600 BCE, the Nubian people's kingdom of Kush in what is now Sudan started to grow in importance. There were power struggles between the Egyptians and Nubians, but by around 750 BCE the Nubians were the most powerful people on the Nile. The Nubians produced fine wall paintings, jewellery, pottery and sculpture.

In around 500 BCE the Nok people in West Africa discovered how to use iron. They melted iron in **furnaces** and used it to make strong tools. These tools helped them to become successful farmers. They also used their furnaces to **fire** dramatic pottery heads. These are the earliest known examples of **terracotta** sculptures in Africa.

Conquerors of the north

Around 330 BCE, North Africa was conquered by the Greeks, and for the next 900 years, it was ruled in turn by Greeks, Romans, **Vandals** and **Byzantines**. However, the invaders who had the most lasting impact on the region were the **Arabs**. Arab armies arrived in northern Africa in 697 CE and 60 years later the region had become part of the **Muslim** Arab Empire.

West African kingdoms and empires

From around 300 CE, a series of powerful empires grew up in West Africa. The most famous of these were the empires of Ghana, Songhai and Mali. Their people mined gold and their rulers became fabulously wealthy by trading with Arab merchants.

Close to the mouth of the river Niger were the rainforest kingdoms of Ife and Benin. Their people were expert potters and metalworkers. Further south, by the mouth of the Congo River, was the kingdom of Kongo, which was famous for its wood carvings of kings.

The Europeans arrive

In 1445, ships from Portugal reached the mouth of the Congo River in West Africa. Soon, traders from many parts of Europe were arriving on the African coast. They bought gold, ivory, iron and slaves from the Africans and sold them weapons, tools, glass and cloth.

In 1652, Dutch traders took over part of southern Africa. But the real scramble for land began in the 19th century. Armies from Europe fought the native African people to win land for themselves, and set up **colonies** all over Africa. The colonial rulers introduced European laws, built European-style buildings and taught the local people to speak their languages. By 1884, only Ethiopia and Liberia were still ruled by Africans.

This bronze portrait of a ruler, or *oni*, was made in the West African kingdom of Ife, some time between the 12th and 15th centuries. It shows the remarkable skill of early African metalworkers.

5000s Sahara starts to turn into desert

3000s Egypt united into one kingdom.

700s Kush people conquer Egypt

500s Nok culture begins

Independence and after

During the 1950s, African countries began to fight for their independence. Between 1960 and 1980 most countries in Africa became independent, but some had to struggle for many years to win their freedom.

Once they had broken free from European rule, many countries still faced huge problems. **Civil wars** broke out in countries such as Nigeria, Angola and Somalia, and wars are still being fought in many parts of Africa. Today, African governments also face problems caused by widespread poverty and by the rapid spread of **AIDS**.

In the period following independence, many African artists broke free from European influences and developed their own styles, based on traditional forms.

The powerful Asante Empire, which flourished in Western Africa in the 18th and 19th centuries, was famous for its goldsmiths.

These engraved golden ornaments would have been worn by Asante rulers, or by officials in the royal court.

CE   600s Arabs invade North Africa

800s Kingdom of Ife begins

1100s Kingdoms of Benin, Ghana and Songhai begin

1200s Kingdom of Mali begins

1350s Kingdom of Great Zimbabwe is at its height

1400s Kingdom of Kongo begins

Africa today

Many Africans today live in towns or cities. Some live in flats or houses, but others struggle to survive in temporary homes in **shantytowns**. However, the majority of Africans still live in the country, in small villages.

African villages usually consist of a group of homes belonging to members of the same extended family. Some villages are run by a chief – the most senior and respected figure in the village. Others are governed by a council of elders – a group of leading figures in the village, who make joint decisions about how things should be run.

Families belong to a larger **ethnic group**, who share the same way of life and usually live in the same area. These people meet together for special ceremonies, such as weddings, funerals and **initiations** – ceremonies to welcome young boys or girls to adult life.

Ancient traditions

People from the same ethnic group often share the same artistic traditions, which are passed down from generation to generation. Many wood carvers, potters and weavers working in Africa today are still using styles and techniques that were first developed thousands of years ago.

This painted wooden figure was carved by artists of the Baoule culture on the coast of West Africa. It shows a European settler wearing a tropical suit and pith helmet.

1450s Portuguese traders arrive in West Africa

1700s Asante Empire begins

1880s European countries colonize much of Africa

1950s African countries start to gain independence

2000s Traditional life continues in villages, but African life in general becomes more influenced by international culture

Rock art

Around 27,000 years ago, people in Africa began to paint pictures on rocks. Stone Age paintings and engravings have been found on rocks and inside caves in many parts of Africa, especially in the Sahara desert and in southern Africa. Many of these early artworks show animals and hunters, and provide a fascinating picture of life in prehistoric Africa. The tradition of painting and carving on rocks has continued through the centuries in desert regions. The Tuareg people of the Sahara still paint pictures of their precious camels on rocks and concrete water tanks in the desert.

The earliest paintings

The rock paintings and engravings found in Africa fall into four distinct groups. The earliest group date from around 25,000 BCE to 6000 BCE, and were created at a time when people survived by hunting. They show wild animals such as elephants, giraffes, rhinos and ostriches – often in incredible detail. Hunters are shown armed with clubs, **throwing-sticks** and arrows, and some of them have very large heads or masks.

These paintings from Tassili, in North Africa, date from the cattle period and show a camp of shepherds with their animals. The figures look elongated and almost cartoon-like.

Changing subjects

Around 6000 BCE, rock artists began to show men as cattle herders as well as hunters. Works from this 'cattle period' are less realistic than earlier examples, with slightly twisted, elongated figures. The 'horse period' began around 1500 BCE. At this time, horses, sheep and dogs started to appear in paintings and engravings, and artists developed a more simplified, **abstract** style.

In paintings of the most recent 'camel period', dating from around 1000 BCE to the present day, desert animals, such as camels and goats, made an appearance. This change in the art reflects what was actually happening in the area, as the grasslands dried up and became desert. The figures in these works are often small and simple, and many of the paintings look almost like diagrams.

These paintings of cattle herders and their animals were made by the San people of the Kalahari Desert in southern Africa. The smaller figures of hunters in the top of the picture were painted at a different time from the larger cattle paintings.

◈ Pigments and brushes

The **pigments** (or paints) used in rock paintings are mainly earth colours – browns, reds, and yellows. These pigments were made from coloured rocks that were ground into a fine powder. The powder was then mixed with blood or egg white to bind it together and to make it stick to the rock. Artists made brushes from hollow bones and sticks, and sometimes used feathers to add details to their paintings.

Architecture

Only a tiny proportion of Africa's ancient buildings survive today. Like most traditional African buildings, they were probably made from mud or wood. The famous walled city of Timbuktu, in the 15th-century kingdom of Mali, was built entirely from mud. It has long since vanished, but medieval travellers described the city and drew its many **mosques**, palaces and homes. The few ancient buildings that do survive, made from stone or rock, show the incredible skill of the early African builders.

Pyramids and temples

Around 2600 BCE the ancient Egyptians began to build stone pyramids in the desert. These massive structures were intended as elaborate tombs for their **pharaohs**. Inside the pyramids a series of tunnels led to a burial chamber. The burial chambers were decorated with paintings and carvings.

The Egyptians also built impressive stone temples along the banks of the Nile.

These temples had tall entranceways, flanked by giant statues. The temples were decorated inside and out with carvings and paintings and outside some of the temples stood tall, needle-like monuments, known as **obelisks**.

The Sphinx and the Great Pyramid were built by the ancient Egyptians on the banks of the River Nile. The Great Pyramid was begun around 2560 BCE and took 20 years to complete. It was constructed from over 2 million blocks of solid stone. The Sphinx is probably much older than the Great Pyramid. It represents a mythical creature, with the body of a lion and the head of a woman.

This church was carved out of solid rock around 1200 CE. Deep below ground level, very little of the church can be seen from the surface. The entranceway shown here leads into a building shaped like a cross.

◈ Building the pyramids

The earliest known pyramid was made from large stone blocks arranged in steep steps. After this, the Egyptians learned the technique of covering the stepped sides of their pyramids with thin sheets of limestone. The smooth, triangular sides of the pyramids were meant to look like the rays of the sun. Nobody knows how the Egyptians planned their pyramids, but they must have used quite advanced mathematics.

Lalibela's churches

Around 1200 CE, King Lalibela of Ethiopia, in northern Africa, gave orders for eleven churches to be carved out of rocks. These extraordinary structures are formed in the shape of a cross. Most of them lie below ground level, so that only the carvings in their roofs are visible from the ground. They are linked by a series of underground tunnels and are still used for services today.

Great Zimbabwe

The walled fortress of Great Zimbabwe was built around 1300 CE. It was the centre of a great southern kingdom that had grown rich from trading in gold. The fortress consisted of a large walled enclosure, and probably contained a palace as well as many smaller, circular buildings. At one end of the fortress was a tall, conical stone tower, which may have been used for religious ceremonies, as a symbol of wealth and power, or possibly for storing grain.

A range of styles

Traditional African homes are built in a vast range of shapes, depending on the materials that people have to build with, and the kinds of shelter they need.

In the rainforests of Central Africa, the Pygmy people build simple, beehive-shaped huts from flexible branches covered with leaves. In the wooded grasslands of the Cameroon, people construct strong, square wooden houses. In dry areas of East Africa, where it hardly ever rains, circular houses with conical (cone-shaped) roofs are made entirely from reeds.

Using mud

One of the most common building materials in Africa is mud or clay. Mud can be easily shaped into bricks, which are dried in the sun and then used to build houses in a wide range of shapes. Mud survives well in hot dry climates, and it can also stand up to heavy rain, so long as it dries out in the sun soon afterwards.

Thick mud walls keep houses cool and can be deep enough to hold spaces that serve as shelves. The Ham people who live around Nok use mud to shape houses that look rather like sculptures, with spaces for storing possessions built into their walls.

Sometimes whole towns in northern Africa are made from mud, strengthened by stones. These towns are often surrounded by high city walls. Inside the walls, there are covered markets, mosques and houses – all built from mud!

The tall houses in this Dogon village, in West Africa, are built into the side of a cliff. Their conical straw roofs are easy to replace and their mud walls can be repaired and renewed each year. Some of the walls are decorated with traditional patterns.

Mosques from mud

In the north and west of Africa, people build magnificent mosques from mud. These large, rectangular buildings are often topped by a series of tall, pyramid-shaped domes. Sometimes the mosques are whitewashed, and the permanent scaffolding posts sticking out from their sides give them a dramatic, prickly appearance.

Renewable buildings

In places with a heavy rainy season, the mud surfaces of buildings have to be 'reskinned' every year. That is why scaffolding posts are left sticking out of many buildings. In Djenne, in West Africa, the whole town gets involved in repairing the mosque, and up to 6000 people complete the massive job in less than a month.

The Great Mosque at Djenne in West Africa was built in 1906, but a mosque has stood on this site since the 13th century. The Great Mosque is one of the wonders of the Muslim world. It is made from sun-dried mud bricks that are plastered over with mud and its walls are more than 0.6 metres (2 feet) thick.

Decorating homes

In many parts of Africa, people paint the outsides of their homes, or carve designs into their smooth mud walls. The Ndebele women of southern Africa paint brightly coloured geometric shapes on to the walls of their whitewashed houses. In Zaria, Nigeria, simple, rectangular homes are often decorated with carvings of modern objects, such as cars, clocks or bicycles. Sometimes the inside walls and floors of mud houses are covered with intricate patterns. These designs vary from one community to another and are often similar to traditional patterns used in body painting.

This village house in the Transvaal area of South Africa has been decorated by Ndebele women. Its whitewashed mud walls are painted with traditional, geometric patterns. The same striking colours and patterns are used in Ndebele jewellery and dress.

Granaries

Most African villages have a granary, where the village grain is stored. These tall, tubular structures are usually made from mud and are protected from the rain by a conical thatched roof. Small openings are left in the side of the granary so grain can be poured in and later collected. Granaries are a sign of a community's wealth and they are often decorated with elaborate carvings.

Houses on stilts

Houses on stilts can be found in several parts of Africa. Raised houses have many advantages. They can be built in thick forests, on swampy ground, on mountain slopes and even in lakes. Raising a house above the ground also helps to protect people from snakes and dangerous animals. Sometimes, the space beneath the house is used for storing food or keeping cattle. In parts of West Africa, whole villages on stilts are built on lakes. The fishing people who live on the lakes use canoes to reach their homes.

Mobile homes

In the dry grasslands of East Africa, people are constantly on the move, searching for water and grazing land for their animals. Most married women in Somalia have their own house – a collection of mats that can be laid over a framework of branches to make a domed tent. When it is time for the family to move on, the house is packed up and carried to the next stopping place.

The tents of the Tuareg people of the Sahara desert are even easier to move around. Their roofs are made from up to 40 animal skins sewn together and supported on wooden poles. The tent walls are made from grass matting which can easily be folded up.

Pottery

People in Africa have been making pots and sculptures from clay for thousands of years. Remains of pots have been found in the Sahara desert that date back more than 7000 years, and by 500 BCE potters from the West African kingdom of Nok were shaping dramatic figures from an orangey-red clay called **terracotta**.

◈ Firing terracotta

Terracotta is a soft clay that can be easily moulded into delicate shapes. The Nok potters used this clay to build up their figures piece by piece. Each part of the figure – head, body, hair and jewellery – was made from a separate piece of clay. Then the potter joined the pieces together and baked the figure over an open fire. The holes in the eyes and nostrils were probably made to allow moisture to escape, and to prevent the pottery from cracking as it was fired.

Figures from Nok

The Nok figures range in size from less than 10 centimetres to almost life-size. Nok statues have large **conical** heads and short, tubular bodies. Their faces are simplified and almost **abstract**, with triangular eyes, wide-lipped mouths and flattened noses. They wear beaded bracelets, necklaces and anklets, all shaped from clay. Archaeologists think the Nok figures may have been placed in **shrines** or buried in graves as offering to gods.

Terracotta figures like this are the earliest African sculptures outside Egypt. Art historians believe that the Nok potters were influenced by masks carved in wood. Modern Yoruba masks show a similar treatment of the face, with flattened, abstract features and pierced holes for eyes.

Ife statues

Around 800 CE, five hundred years after the kingdom of Nok disappeared, the powerful kingdom of Ife grew up in the same area. Potters from Ife made fine terracotta statues. Like the Nok figures, the Ife statues have conical heads and short bodies, but their heads are remarkably detailed and **naturalistic**. Ife was ruled by a series of kings called *onis*, and the terracotta statues were probably portraits of *onis*. In addition to these portrait figures, potters from Ife also made much more abstract human figures as well as realistic sculptures of animals.

Terracotta traditions

Many West African kingdoms have produced fine examples of terracotta sculpture. Between the 14th and 16th centuries, potters around the city of Djenne created **stylized** human figures, often shown crouching with their heads raised high, as if appealing for help. Some of the figures have snakes or other reptiles crawling over them.

Potters working today around the village of Nok make terracotta figures to use as ornaments, called finials, on the roofs of their buildings. These modern figures are part of a long tradition of terracotta sculpture in West Africa.

This Djenne figurine has a crouching posture and an uplifted face. This stylized gesture of appeal is found on many pieces from this region.

Traditional water pots

The basic shape of the African water pot has remained the same for centuries. Its completely rounded shape allows it to be set down at any angle in a dip in the ground. It can fit comfortably inside a head ring or against the shoulder of the person who is carrying it. The pot's small neck prevents water from leaking out.

Many pots have striations (scored marks) around the top to make them easy to grip. Pots are often only partially **glazed**, so that some water can evaporate through the sides of the pot and the water inside can stay cool.

Berber amphorae

Berber women from northern Africa make and carry tall, elegant water jugs, known as amphorae. These slender, two-handled water carriers look strikingly similar to pots made in Mediterranean countries thousands of years ago. Storage jars like these must have been brought to North Africa by Greek traders around 300 BCE.

The amphorae are hand-built from coils of clay. Then they are polished smooth with stones and varnished before being painted. Painted designs on amphorae usually include bands of zigzags and triangles. A pair of raised circles, resembling eyes, and a simplified hand are often included in the designs. The hand is the 'hand of Fatima', daughter of the prophet Muhammad. Together, the eye and hand symbols are believed to keep away the spirit of evil, known as the 'evil eye'.

These pots, for sale in a North African market, have been left unglazed. The water pots in the foreground have been painted with traditional patterns, using charcoal.

◇ Making pots

Most African pots are built by hand using the 'coil pot' method. A lump of clay is placed in the centre of a shallow, rounded mould and smoothed into shape. Then coils of clay are added to this base and wound round and round to build up the sides of the pot. As the pot grows, the potter pinches and pulls at the clay to make the sides thinner and flatter. Sometimes a banana leaf is placed between the mould and the base of the pot to stop the base from drying out too quickly and to make it easier to release the finished pot.

Body art and adornment

In many African cultures, people decorate their bodies. They may paint patterns on their faces and bodies, create elaborate hairstyles, make a permanent design of scars on their skin, or even alter their body shape. In south-east Nigeria, where fatness is admired, young girls spend some time in a fattening house before they are **initiated** into adult womanhood. In Kenya, Kikuyu women wear **earplugs** (flat, round earrings covering and stretching the lower part of the ear) because extended earlobes are considered beautiful.

Body painting

Body painting is especially important to the herders of East Africa, whose wandering lifestyle does not allow them to create many permanent works of art. Young Nuban men from Sudan decorate their bodies to attract a wife. They paint their heads with bold blocks of white, black, red and blue colour, and decorate their faces and bodies with **abstract** patterns of swirls, triangles and dots. This painting can take hours to complete, and has to be constantly renewed, as the Nubans bathe daily.

The Maasai herders of Kenya rub a mixture of red **ochre** and oil into their skin to make their bodies shine. They also rub ochre into their hair, which is braided into elaborate styles. Young Maasai men apply ochre when they go out hunting and for ceremonial dances. They also use it to make themselves look handsome to attract young women.

Sometimes, body paint is worn to ward off danger. The Pygmy people of the Central African rainforest paint designs on their faces to keep themselves safe from evil spirits. In parts of North and West Africa, an orange dye made from the henna plant is used to paint intricate patterns on the hands, feet and face. It is not only used to make people look beautiful but also to protect them against evil.

Scarification

The art of making patterns of scars on the body is called **scarification**. It is mainly practised in Africa by the Nuba, Nuer and Mossi people.

The Mossi people of Burkina Faso originally used facial scarring to mark the faces of boys who were not allowed to be sold into slavery. They used a method in which a small amount of skin was removed in order to create a dip in the skin.

Young Nuba girls are given a pattern of raised scars over their upper bodies. The scars are made over several years, from **puberty** to the time of the birth of their first child. The scars mark a young woman's gradual change in status from a girl to a woman, and are considered beautiful.

Nowadays, the practice of scarification is dying out. Many people see it as cruel, and young Africans who may not spend their whole lives in their villages, no longer wish to have their faces and bodies marked.

Maasai warriors from East Africa decorate their bodies with stripes and traditional patterns for their ceremonial dances. They also wear beads and elaborate headdresses as part of their total body art.

Hairstyles

Hairstyles in Africa are very important for showing a person's position in society, and styles often change as a child becomes an adult and then gets married. Hairstyles can even be used to show what job a person does.

Usually, the size of a hairstyle indicates the importance of its wearer. The wives of Shona rulers and chiefs have enormous, elaborate hairstyles which take hours to create and need to be carefully protected at night.

In some African societies, beards are a way of showing a man's status, with grey beards being especially prized because they indicate age, intelligence and wisdom.

Jewellery

Most Africans wear some sort of jewellery as part of their traditional dress. They may wear necklaces, armbands, anklets and earrings. They may also have beads braided into their hair or wear elaborate headdresses.

In many African cultures, jewellery is a sign of wealth. Items of jewellery are passed from one generation to the next and precious items may be stored in family chests and only brought out for special occasions.

Many materials

Jewellery may be made from metal, or carved from wood or ivory. Beads, shells, coral and leather can all be used to make jewellery. The San women of the Kalahari desert make tiny beads from broken pieces of ostrich eggshells. These beads are used to decorate the borders of clothes and headbands. The Himba cattle herders of southern Africa wear necklaces made from cattle horns and even cattle ears.

Berber silver

The Berber women of North Africa wear masses of heavy, silver jewellery that clinks and glints in the sun as they walk. As well as wearing necklaces, headdresses and earrings, they also use elaborate clasps, called fibulae, to hold their cloaks together. Hanging from their necklaces, headdresses and fibulae are many silver coins. The silver indicates to others the wealth of an individual, and is regarded as a status symbol.

Modern materials

Today, modern materials are often used in jewellery. Artists use plastic-covered electrical wire, buttons and bottle tops in their traditional designs for necklaces and headdresses. In parts of South Africa, women wear circular earplugs that are cut from vinyl floor tiles.

Fulani gold

Fulani women from north-west Africa wear enormous, circular earrings made from beaten gold. The earrings can be so large that the woman has to wear a string over her head to help support their weight. As a woman's husband's wealth increases, more gold is beaten into her earrings and they become even larger.

This young Fulani woman is wearing traditional jewellery. As well as her headdress, nosering and necklaces, she wears enormous earrings made from beaten gold. In many traditional African societies, the amount of jewellery that a woman wears is a sign of her family's wealth.

Beadwork

Glass beads were first made by the ancient Egyptians, but European beads were brought to Africa by Italian merchants in the 16th century. Nowadays, people in many parts of Africa use glass and plastic beads to make necklaces, headbands, and many other items of clothing and jewellery.

The Maasai women of Kenya wear colourful headbands, earrings, bracelets and necklaces all made from beads. The Dinka people of the Sudan make elaborate beaded garments which fit like corsets around their bodies. In Nigeria, the Yoruba people make beaded hats, fans and boots to be worn by their king.

Beaded aprons

In south-east Africa, Ndebele women sew beads on to goatskin to make patterned aprons. The design of these aprons varies depending on the age of the wearer. When a girl comes of age, she wears a large apron, with arm and ankle bracelets that she has made herself. When she gets married, she wears a bridal apron that is partly made by her mother-in-law. After the birth of her first child, she is allowed to wear a married woman's apron. Ndebele bridal aprons have a fringe made up of broad strips. These strips represent the cattle that the bridegroom's family pays for his bride.

Maasai women wear necklaces, bracelets, earrings and sometimes even hats made from strands of glass and plastic beads. Beaded necklaces can be extremely heavy, but their many strands are a sign of a woman's high status.

The bead aprons of the Ndebele women clearly indicate the stage of life that their wearer has reached. In many African cultures, clothing and jewellery are used to show the status of their wearer. This also happens in modern Western culture, where wedding dresses are worn to signify a woman's transition into marriage and wedding rings display married status.

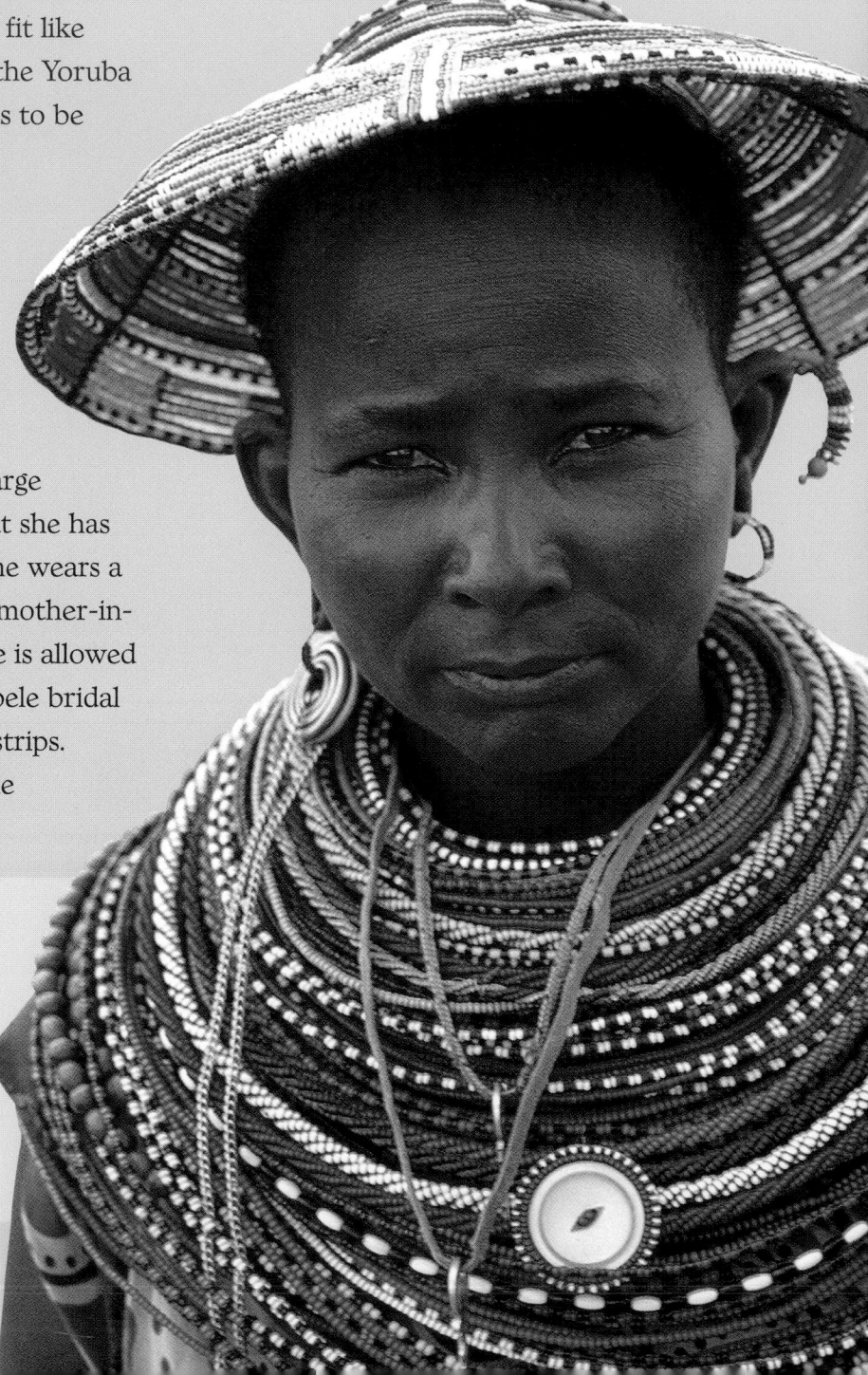

This Zulu dancer is wearing a glorious jumble of beaded necklaces. The colours and patterns used in some traditional Zulu necklaces have a special significance (see box below).

Necklaces with a message

In parts of southern Africa, beaded jewellery is used to send messages. Zulu girls weave necklaces of white beads with **pendants** hanging down from them made from different coloured beads. Each colour has a special meaning and together the colours make up a message that can be read. The girls send necklaces to boys that they love. Sometimes boys wear several love messages at the same time.

◈ The language of beads

The colours used in Zulu love necklaces each have a special meaning, but these meanings can vary. Red stands for love, anger or pain, white for purity or truth, and black for disappointment. Blue can mean faithfulness, the sea or gossip, but it can also be used to make a request. Green stands for grass or loneliness, and yellow for home and wealth. Yellow also represents cow dung and can be used as an insult!

Textiles

African **textile** makers use a vast range of different materials to make their cloth. In the rainforests of Central Africa, people make textiles from trees and plants. They use bark from trees to make strong cloth. They also weave **fibres** from **raffia** palms, pineapple leaves and bamboo plants.

Bark cloth

Bark cloth was probably the first type of cloth that humans made. It is still made by the Mbuti people who live around the Congo River. The bark comes from the pongo tree. When the inner layer of bark is scraped away, a layer of tissue known as the bast is left behind. This is pounded with a bone mallet for about two days until the material is soft and all the sap has escaped. Then it is dried in the sun for five to six days.

Once the bast is thoroughly dry, it can be painted. The Mbuti use a blackish-blue **pigment** that is made by crushing charcoal and mixing it with the juice of gardenia flowers. The paintings are usually **geometric**, **abstract** shapes. Broader lines are made with fingers dipped in paint. Finer ones are applied with a twig or a plant stem. The decorated bark cloth is worn by women as aprons and by men as **loincloths**.

Using raffia

Raffia fibres come from the raffia palm, which has wide, flat leaves. The leaves are stripped away, leaving just the stem, which is dried in the sun. Raffia fibres are used to make a range of useful things such as ropes, baskets, mats and traps for catching animals. They can also be woven into squares of fabric and the squares can be stitched together to make larger pieces of cloth.

Cut-pile

Sometimes raffia cloth has patterns stitched into it. This kind of decorated raffia is known as **cut-pile**. The Kuba people of the Congo make a famous cut-pile cloth known as Kasai velvet. First, a base is woven from fibres of raffia. Then raffia threads are stitched in different patterns on to the base. The threads are cut off close to the surface, creating a texture rather like velvet. Kasai velvets are usually coloured beige – the natural colour of raffia – with geometric patterns in black. The cloth is used to make robes, cushions and bags, and is an essential element of Kuba ceremonial dress.

This Kuba man is weaving raffia fibre on a loom. He sits on a raffia mat and is wearing a small cap made from raffia and decorated with traditional patterns.

Decorating cloth

Throughout the continent of Africa, weavers produce cloth from cotton, wool or silk. But in each area, people have developed different ways of adding pattern and decoration to their cloth. Some weave patterns into the cloth, some dye it in exciting ways, using **tie-dye** techniques or printing patterns on to its surface. Traditional cloth-makers often use embroidery or appliqué work to add an extra layer of decoration to their cloth.

Strips of cloth

In many West African societies, it is the men who do the weaving, and boys begin practising on miniature looms at an early age. Unlike women weavers, who usually work on wide looms, the men have narrow looms that can easily be moved from place to place. They produce long strips of cloth that are later sewn together to create a broad piece of cloth. The most well-known strip cloths are known as Kente and are woven by the Akan people of Ghana. Kente cloths are made up of bold, multicoloured strips.

Factory-printed cloth

Perhaps the most widespread form of cloth found in Africa today is factory-printed cloth. This was originally imported from Europe but it is now largely made in Africa. Designs for factory-printed cloth may show famous figures, such as world cup footballers, current events, or contemporary objects, like mobile phones and computers.

Some of the factory-cloth designs have special meanings. For example, one pattern is a reminder not to gossip about others. It can be worn to scold a person, such as an elder, who could not be told off in any other way.

Kente cloth is woven in narrow strips like this, and then sewn together. The striped pattern is typical of Kente designs.

Using appliqué

Appliqué is the technique of stitching cut-out designs on to a larger piece of cloth. It is often used to create banners that are carried at special ceremonies, such as weddings or funerals. The West African kingdom of Dahomey, which flourished in the 19th century, was famous for its appliqué work. Only male members of the royal court were allowed to sew designs on to banners and royal umbrellas. Most of the designs showed great battles.

This colourful banner was made in the village of Ganvie, near Benin in West Africa. Like many appliqué banners, it features images of local animals, plants and insects.

◈ Yoruba patterns

Yoruba women from Nigeria wear dresses made from brightly-coloured cotton cloth, which they dye using natural dyes, such as indigo. Before they dye the cloth, they paint designs on to it, using a paste made from the roots of the cassava plant. The areas that are covered with paste do not absorb the dye. Each pattern has a special meaning. The women get ideas for designs from things around them, such as birds or plants, or from local sayings.

Masks

Masks are worn in many African cultures during important ceremonies, such as marriages, funerals and **initiations**. They can also be used to teach people about their history, or to discipline someone who has disobeyed the rules of their community. Masks are usually worn as part of a total costume, including jewellery and body painting.

Different materials

African masks are often made from wood, and then painted or carved with traditional designs. However, mask makers may use a wide range of different materials, including animal skins, **raffia**, feathers and beads. The Kuba people of the Congo, in Central Africa, decorate royal masks with brass, leather, beads and precious cowrie shells.

Women's masks

Masks are usually worn by men, but Mende women of the women's societies of Sierre Leone wear masks. Senior members of the society wear wooden masks, called *sowei*, to celebrate the time when young girls become women and join the society. The masks have thin eyes, high foreheads, pointed chins and rolls of fat around the neck – all signs of beauty in the Mende culture.

Animal masks

Many African masks resemble human faces, but some are designed to look like animals. Some masks made by the Makonde people of East Africa look like long-eared hares, while the Do people of the Côte d'Ivoire carve masks with large, curved beaks like birds. A dancer wearing an animal mask will often perform an athletic dance to represent the movements of that animal.

A Mende *sowei* mask, seen from the side. Masks like this are worn by Mende women at initiation ceremonies, to welcome young girls into their society. With its rolls of fat and high forehead, the mask repesents an ideal of female beauty in the Mende culture.

Having fun

Sometimes masks are simply used to entertain. The Yoruba people have a masked dance, or **masquerade**, that humorously depicts foreigners and their strange dress and manners. The Dogon people hold similar masquerades showing Westerners and their strange ways. One of the dancers wears a mask representing an anthropologist (someone who studies **ethnic groups**) and walks around with a pen and paper asking people silly questions!

Funeral masks

Dogon dancers wear high wooden helmet masks for their ceremonial dances to mourn the dead. The dancers perform a complicated dance, rising and dipping to the rhythm of the drums. They take huge leaps into the air and plunge down so low that their masks sweep the ground.

This Maasai carver from East Africa is preparing a mask for final carving. A finished mask is propped up behind him. The masks will be used in ceremonial dances.

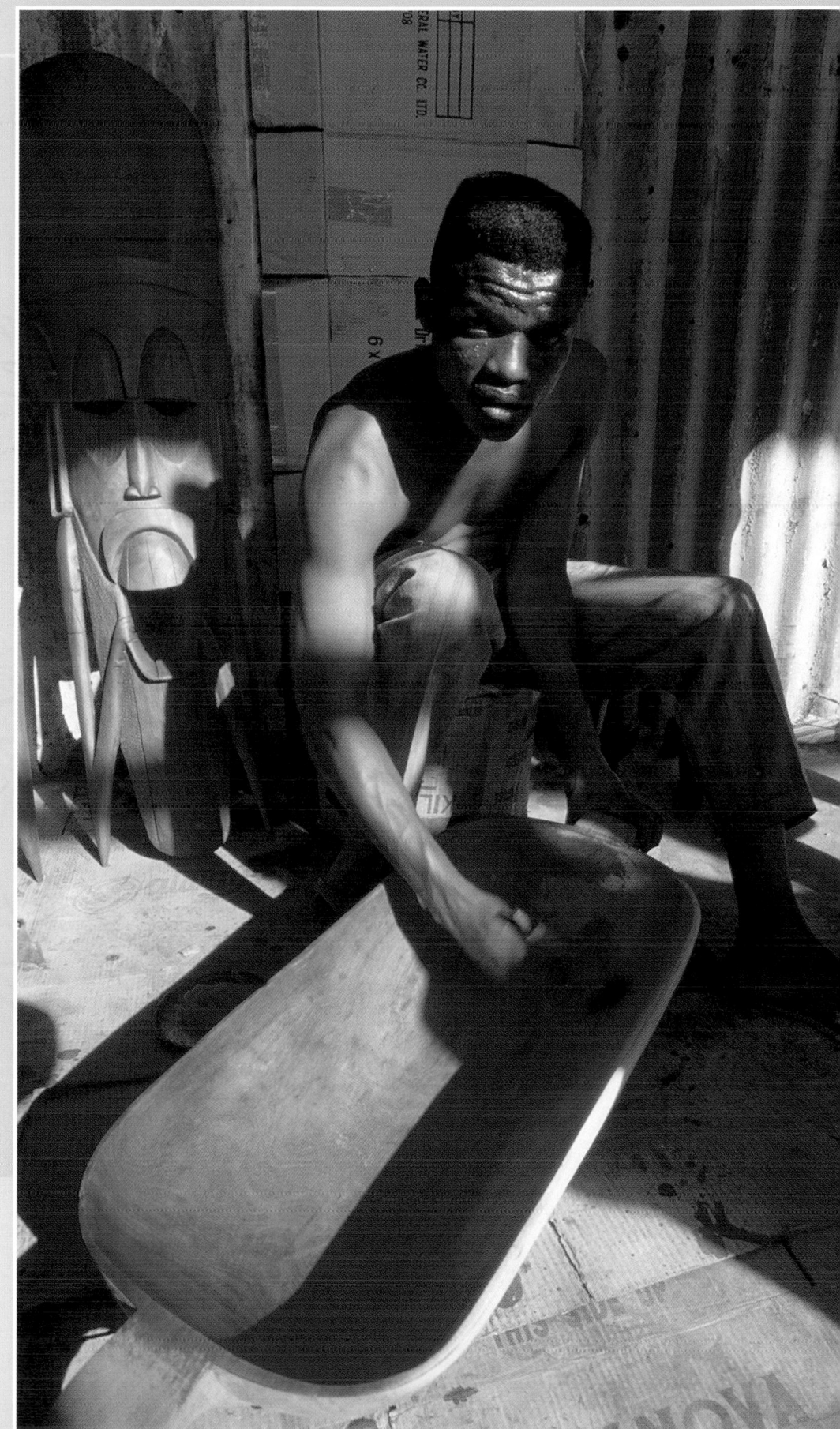

33

Wood carving

Wood is extremely important in African art. It is used for carving masks, statues and musical instruments and for making domestic objects such as furniture and bowls. It is also used to make weapons such as spears, bows and shields.

In some Central African cultures, the wood carver has a special role. There may be an official village carver who is expected to retire when his apprentice takes over. The training to become a carver may take many years, and has religious as well as practical aspects.

Headrests

The wandering herders of the East African grasslands do not have many possessions, so portable items of furniture, such as headrests, are very precious. Headrests were traditionally used to support a sleeping person's neck and were especially useful for preserving elaborate hairstyles and stopping them from being damaged during sleep. Headrests are no longer used every night, but the Shona people believe that if a man sleeps with his neck on a headrest, it will encourage vivid dreams and help the dreamer to make contact with his ancestors. Each Shona man has his own headrest, which he keeps for his whole life. Sometimes headrests are buried with their owner and sometimes they are handed down to a son.

Headrests are usually carved from a single tree trunk. The circles, lines and triangle patterns carved on Shona headrests are very similar to the **scarification** marks of Shona women. Luba carvers sometimes carve two kneeling figures supporting the headrest.

Drinking cups

The Lele wood carvers of the Congo make and decorate drums, hunting bows, bellows and bowls, but they are best known for their elaborate drinking cups. Some cups are decorated with geometric patterns and some are carved in the form of a human head. Often, the more elaborate the carving is, the more important the owner is in their society. The double-headed drinking cup is considered especially precious. Only a really skilled carver can make a double cup out of a single block of wood so that the liquid flows both ways. The Lele carvers of the Congo work with a soft wood that can be carved with knives and soft iron gouges. The carved objects are then hardened and blackened by hanging them from roof beams over a fire.

◈ Carving and treating wood

Most African sculptures are carved from a single piece of hardwood, that can last for a long time and has no joins to work loose. First the object is carved out roughly from a piece of wood, using a small axe, known as an adze. Then it is polished until it is very smooth.

Sometimes, details are carved with the adze, but a carver may also use a knife or a chisel. The sculpture may then be stained or painted. It may also be decorated by burning lines on to its surface – a technique known as pyro-engraving.

This headrest is carved from a single block of wood by the Shona people of Zimbabwe.

Carved stools

Wooden stools are made all over Africa in an amazing variety of styles. They are usually decorated with figures and animals or abstract patterns. Stools are used in everyday life, but elaborate ceremonial stools are made for kings and chiefs.

Asante ceremonial stools have crescent-shaped seats and are decorated with beads or copper nails. Because the stool is understood to be the seat of the owner's soul, it is leaned against a wall when it is not in use so that other passing souls will not settle on it.

Ceremonial stools made by the Bamileke people of the Cameroon grasslands have carvings of leopards, human figures and spiders. The spider is a symbol of wisdom, while the leopard symbolizes power and strength. Perhaps the most famous ceremonial stools are those carved by the Luba people. Their seats are supported by a carved female figure, symbolizing the important role of the mother in Luba society.

Gods, ancestors and kings

Throughout Africa, wood carvers create dramatic figures of gods, ancestors and spirits. These figures can be enormous, such as the towering memorial posts erected by the Konso people of Ethiopia in honour of the dead heroes of their community. They can also be small-scale – figures to be placed on altars in shrines, or buried in the graves of chiefs. Carved wooden figures of ancestors are often placed on the roofs of a chief's hut or on land around a village. These figures are intended to protect the villagers from harm.

In many African kingdoms, there is a tradition of carving royal figures. Some of the most well-known royal statues are those made by the Kuba people from the Congo. Kuba figures are dignified and graceful, with **idealized**, perfect features. The eyes are closed, suggesting that the king can communicate with the world beyond. These figures were usually carved at the time of the king's coronation and kept as a memorial figure – a reminder of the king's presence after his death.

Carved door posts

In some West African cultures, important buildings such as **shrines** and the houses of chiefs, have carved wooden door posts. The posts are sometimes covered with patterns, but often they show a figure, such as a hunter, the wife of the king, or the king himself. Sometimes such figures play a role as guardians, keeping the building safe. But more often, these figures remind visitors to the building about the roles of leaders and others in society. They may also remind people of historical persons, myths, gods or spirits.

Young Kikuyu warriors wear painted wooden shields like this in their ceremonial dances. The shield is attached by an armband to a boy's upper arm.

Kikuyu shields

Many African shields are made from wood, which is sometimes covered in animal hide and sometimes painted. Today, shields are mainly used in ceremonies and dances. Kikuyu boys in Kenya wear wooden dance shields on their upper arms when they are welcomed into the society of adult men. The shields are carved from lightweight wood and are mainly oval-shaped. They are often decorated with black and white zigzag patterns. The patterns probably represent the rugged snow-capped summit of Mount Kenya (considered by the Kikuyu to be a sacred mountain).

Fantasy coffins

A new type of wood carving has recently been developed by the Ga people, in southern Ghana. Here, skilled carvers make coffins in special shapes from painted wood. So, a dairy farmer may order a coffin shaped like a giant milk carton and a fisherman may have a coffin that looks like a fish. This new tradition of 'fantasy coffins' began when a fisherman asked his nephew to help him make a fish-shaped coffin because he hoped to be able to go fishing in the next world.

The skilled carving on Ghanaian fantasy coffins illustrates the range of possibilities available; from hens to rowing boats, the only limit is the imagination of the artist.

Metalwork

Around 1200 CE, metalworkers in the West African kingdom of Ife discovered a way to cast figures in bronze. For the next 300 years, court metalworkers at Ife produced exquisite bronze sculptures. The tradition of casting metal figures was continued in the neighbouring kingdom of Benin, where it lasted until the 1890s.

Ife heads

Many of the surviving Ife bronzes are portraits of rulers, known as *onis*. These portrait heads are strikingly realistic, with perfect proportions. The *onis* are shown as calm and dignified, gazing straight ahead. The statues have a smooth, polished finish and rows of holes are pierced around the head and sometimes the beard areas. Art historians think that these areas may have been covered by a veil of beads.

Around the base of the bronze heads are more holes, but rather than holding beads, these were possibly used to attach the bronze heads to wooden bodies. The statues may have been dressed in the crown and royal clothing of a deceased *oni* and used in important religious ceremonies.

Bronzes from Benin

Bronze casting in Benin lasted from the 15th century to the 19th century and during that time sculptors moved from **naturalistic** portraits, like the figures at Ife, to a much more **abstract** style.

The most famous Benin bronzes are the portraits of rulers (known as *obas*) and queen mothers (known as *iyobas*) made in the 16th century. These heads have strong, simplified features and are less naturalistic than the Ife portraits. Metalworkers from Benin also produced realistic sculptures of animals and flat plaques, with raised figures and scenes.

This graceful bronze portrait of a queen mother was made in the kingdom of Benin in the late 16th century CE.

These boys are using the ancient lost wax method to create small craft items for sale. This lengthy method of producing bronzes can also be found in other cultures, including India, where it is a respected skill.

◈ The lost wax process

The process is a complicated technique, which requires great patience and skill. First, a rough model of the final sculpture is made in clay. This is known as the core. Then a layer of beeswax is applied over the core. The beeswax is carefully moulded into shape, and extra strips of decoration are added using a moulding stick. When the beeswax model is finished, it is covered with three layers of clay, to form a clay mould, with a hole in its base so the wax can run out. The clay mould is then fired, and the wax melts away. Molten (liquid) bronze is poured into the empty mould and left to cool. Once the metal is completely cool, the clay mould is broken open and the metal sculpture can be taken out and polished. Only at this final stage, does the sculptor know if the process has been a success.

African gold

Africa is rich in gold. Gold was used by the Egyptians and was first mined in West Africa around the 4th century CE. The early West African goldsmiths made ceremonial jewellery and ornaments but very little of this work survives. Objects made from gold were often seized by European settlers, or melted down by Africans so that they could sell the gold for high prices to **Arab** and European merchants.

Akan goldsmiths

The Akan people of Ghana are famous for their work in gold. They are descended from the people of the great Asante Empire, which flourished in the 18th and 19th centuries. The symbol of the Asante Empire was a wooden stool covered in sheets of gold, which is said to have fallen from Heaven when the empire was founded. For their ceremonies, Akan chiefs wear golden pectorals (disks covering their chests) and headdresses.

Akan goldsmiths decorate the handles of ceremonial swords and make **stylized** ornaments in the shape of crocodiles, fish, birds and other naturalistic or abstract forms. The surfaces of all these works are covered in delicate carvings and gold filigree (fine threads of gold).

This stylized statue shows a warrior riding a horse. Solid gold ornaments like this were used by West African merchants from the 14th century onwards. The merchants used the ornaments as weights to measure the value of the gold dust they were buying.

Silversmiths from Ethiopia make crosses in a wide range of traditional designs. Ethiopian Christians wear crosses on a cord called a *mateb,* which is given to them when they are baptized.

◈ Animal proverbs

Animals often feature in the work of the Akan goldsmiths. These creatures have special meanings because of the traditional proverbs or sayings associated with them. For example, a snake is associated with the proverb 'A snake bites when it is angry' and it is a reminder not to rouse the chief's anger, while a stretched-out frog reminds people that 'The full length of a frog only appears when it is dead.' This proverb teaches that a person's true worth cannot be judged in their lifetime.

Ethiopian silver

Ethiopia has a long tradition of work in silver. For over 1600 years, Christians in Ethiopia have worn silver crosses around their necks as a symbol of their faith, and large silver crosses are still carried today in religious processions. Each region has its own design, which can vary from a simple crucifix shape, with one or two crossbars, to a much more elaborate design. Many Ethiopian crosses are made from interwoven strips of silver that are meant to symbolize eternity.

Baskets, gourds and eggshells

The Tutsi women of Rwanda are famous for their coil-sewn baskets. These elegant patterned baskets come in many sizes and are often crowned with a **conical** lid. They are made from strands of grass wrapped in thinly-cut strips of banana leaf to form a continuous coil which is sewn together.

Most Tutsi baskets are decorated with regular geometric patterns in dark brown or black. Their precisely worked out patterns require very careful planning. Some of the designs create dramatic and surprising visual effects, as they spiral up the baskets.

Calabash covers

Calabashes are tall, long-necked **gourds**, that are dried and hollowed out and used as containers. The Tutsi people use them to store banana wine. They are topped with basketwork covers to keep out dust and flies. Over the years, the calabash covers made by the Tutsi women have became important objects in their own right, and they are now created as free-standing sculptures. These tall baskets appear to be half human and half animal, with a funnel-shaped body crowned by a pair of horns.

At this market Tutsi craftspeople sell their bowls and baskets. Each piece has a distinctive geometric pattern in strong, dark colours.

A San artist decorates a water bottle made from the shell of an ostrich egg. First, the outlines of a design are carved into the shell and then charcoal is rubbed into the shapes. The simplified cattle drawn on this bottle are similar to cattle shown in San rock paintings (see page 11).

Gourds and eggshells

Gourds are used all over Africa for carrying and storing water, milk, food stuffs, wine or medicines, as well as being used as food bowls, cups or spoons. Usually, they are left plain, but sometimes they are carved with geometric patterns and coloured with plant dyes.

The San people of the Kalahari desert use the shells of ostrich eggs as water carriers and sometimes carve simple designs on them. The shapes are carved with a knife and then ash or charcoal is rubbed into them to make them stand out strongly against the white eggshell. Fragments of eggshell bottles have been found in the Kalahari dating back more than 12,000 years. Some of them were decorated with animals and human figures.

◈ Making an ostrich eggshell water bottle

It takes a San woman about an hour to prepare an eggshell for use. She drills a small hole in the shell, shakes out its contents and cleans the inside with herbs. Then she makes a small grass stopper. The shells are about the size of a large cantaloupe melon and hold approximately a litre of water. They are not easily broken and can last for several years.

43

Musical instruments

All over Africa, music and dance play a vital part in marking important events, such as births, marriages and deaths. The people of Africa have created an astonishing variety of musical instruments, which are used in different combinations to create a vast range of sounds. As well as producing a great sound, the instruments are also works of art. They may be carved into surprising shapes, covered with patterns, and decorated with beads, feathers, paint or cloth.

In addition to the all-important drums, which provide the rhythm for dances and chants, African instrument-makers also create xylophones, flutes, horns and pipes, and a range of stringed instruments. Bells, gongs, rattles and clappers are often used to add extra sounds and rhythms.

Different drums

Traditional drums are made from wood and animal skins, from the hard shells of fruit, or from **gourds**. They can range in size from small hand-drums to huge ceremonial drums that are almost as tall as the drummer.

Many African drums are made from hollowed-out wood with an animal skin stretched over it to make a **membrane** that the drummer taps. Some drums have a single membrane, which is stretched over the top of the drum and secured by pegs.

Other drums have two membranes – one at the top and one at the bottom that are attached to each other by many strings.

Yoruba talking drums are tall and goblet-shaped with two membranes joined together by strings. The player skillfully squeezes the strings while beating one end of the drum. This produces high and low sounds, which sound like talking in the Yoruba language. Yoruba talking drums are often grouped in 'families' of three, with a large 'mother drum', a medium-sized drum, and a 'baby drum'. The drummers communicate by calling to each other and then responding, creating a 'praise poem' in honour of the gods.

Some 'hourglass drums' can be tucked under the player's arm. By squeezing the strings with his arm, the player can tighten or loosen the membranes at either end of the drum and change the note made by the drum.

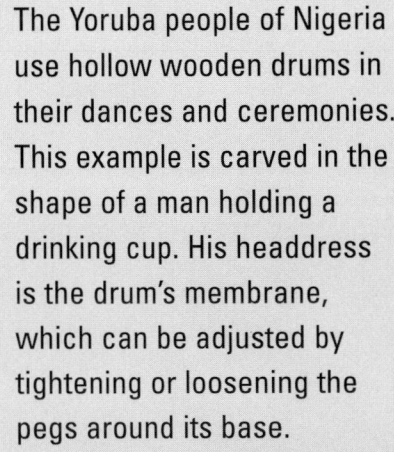

The Yoruba people of Nigeria use hollow wooden drums in their dances and ceremonies. This example is carved in the shape of a man holding a drinking cup. His headdress is the drum's membrane, which can be adjusted by tightening or loosening the pegs around its base.

A Samburu man from East Africa plays an instrument made from a kudu horn. (A kudu is a type of antelope.)

Side-blown trumpets

Trumpets have several different uses. In many parts of Africa, they are used to send messages between villages or between groups of herders, while in some Islamic areas a trumpeter summons people to prayer. One of the most unusual African trumpets is the side-blown trumpet of the Madi people in Uganda. It is made from strips of leather wrapped around wood and the mouthpiece, on the side of the instrument, is made from a piece of gourd.

◈ Musical materials

Traditional instruments are often made from wood, leather and gourds, but music makers are constantly creating new instruments from surprising materials, such as metal fencing, tin cans and bottle tops.

Musical bows

Musical bows are made in the Cameroons. They consist of a simple wooden stick with several strings tightly stretched across it. The strings can be plucked, struck or played with a bow (like a violin). Hollowed-out gourds are attached to the top of the musical bow and act as **resonators**, making the sounds produced by the strings louder and stronger. A skilled musician can produce a wide range of sounds from the bow by holding it at different angles against his body.

Lutes and lyres

Lutes are stringed instruments rather like a guitar. They have a set of strings attached to a long neck and stretched over a hollow resonator. The people of Mali make elegant lutes known as *koras*, with very long necks. The resonator is made from a gourd cut in half and covered by a tightly-stretched cow skin. The musician rests the gourd against his body and plucks the strings with his thumbs and forefingers.

Lyres have their strings attached to a horizontal crossbar. They were used by the ancient Nubians, who lived in what is now Sudan, and the tradition of making and playing lyres still continues in Sudan today. Sudanese lyres are called *rebabas*, because of the gentle sound that they make. They are often hung with beads, shells and coins. *Rebabas* are played by shepherds and goatherds and are popular at weddings.

Thumb pianos

Thumb pianos or *sanzas* work like a tiny hand-held piano, with narrow wooden or metal strips acting as keys. The keys are fixed to a resonator made from hollowed-out wood or a gourd. Musicians use their thumbs to pluck the strips which each produce a different note. The *sanza* is sometimes called the 'traveller's friend' because people can play it while they are on the move.

Sanzas are one of the most ancient of African instruments. They are known to have existed as early as 1000 BCE, and singers have used thumb pianos for centuries to accompany their love ballads.

Sometimes thumb pianos are carved in the shape of a human figure. The Zande people who live on the borders of Sudan and the Congo specialize in making *sanzas* that are shaped like dancing women.

This wooden harp was carved by the Azande people of Central Africa. It has a stylized human shape, with a very long neck, a small head and a wide body. The harp strings are adjusted by turning the pegs on the instrument's neck.

Stringed harps

Carved wooden harps are often used to accompany storytelling. The harps are used in court life but also by travelling musicians. The Mangbetu and Azande people of Central Africa make wonderfully expressive harps in the shape of human bodies, with a long, bendy neck and a wide body, to which the strings are attached.

Cross-currents

In the course of their long history, the people of Africa have been in contact with many different nations. In particular, the **Arab** traders and settlers, who arrived in Africa in the 7th century CE and the Europeans, who ruled most of Africa in the 19th century, have both left their mark on African art and culture.

More recently, Western-style television and advertising have now reached most parts of Africa. All of these influences have had an effect on African art, but artists have nevertheless maintained many of their own traditions, while incorporating new styles, subjects and media into their art.

Arab influences

The influence of Arabic art and culture can be seen throughout North Africa, and also in parts of West Africa, where the Arabs had strong trading links. In the North African countries of Morocco, Tunisia, Algeria and Egypt, people produce embroidery, jewellery, glassware and carpets that are strongly influenced by Arabic and **Persian** traditions. They build **mosques** with domed roofs and minarets and produce illuminated manuscripts of sacred Islamic texts.

European influences

Very soon after the Portuguese arrived in Africa, they began to **commission** African artists to create works that appealed to European tastes. During the 15th and 16th centuries, West African ivory workers carved saltcellars, spoons, forks and dagger handles for the Portuguese. These surprising works show figures with European features and clothes, and include designs and patterns that were clearly influenced by Western art.

This intricate saltcellar was carved in Sierra Leone in the 16th century. It was made for Portuguese traders and shows both African and European figures.

In this painting, *Ana Angali Wa Uvimbe* (1991), the artist Georges Lilanga di Nyama combines startling modern effects with traditional elements such as cartoon-like figures.

In the 19th century, many African cloth makers were encouraged to abandon their traditional designs in favour of European patterns of birds and flowers. Meanwhile, some Africans began to wear European clothing. Today, many people in Africa wear a combination of traditional African and Western-style dress, often using Western clothes in inventive ways.

African artists today

Today, artists across Africa work in a wide variety of media, from painting and printmaking to **ceramics**, **textiles**, sculpture and photography. Many contemporary African artists use Western styles and techniques, but rely on African traditions and images as the inspiration for their work. The sculptor Sokari Douglas Camp draws on memories of her childhood in Nigeria to create dramatic steel sculptures, including a vast kinetic (moving) sculpture in memory of her father, based on a traditional Kalabari funeral bed. The Ethiopian Alexander Boghossian creates paintings based on ancient Ethiopian scrolls and the Tunisian Nja Mahdaoui uses Islamic script in his 'calligrams'. Some artists use specifically African materials – the Nigerian artist Jimoh Buraimoh creates colourful mosaics from beads and shells, while Yinka Shonibare makes 'soft sculptures' from African printed cloth. Recent African history is also a popular subject. The Egyptian Chant Avedissian assembles collages of life in Cairo during the 1950s, while a number of South African artists create powerful images of the conflict between blacks and whites.

49

Early reactions

When Portuguese traders first arrived in West Africa, in the 1400s, they were amazed at the fine examples of pottery and metalwork that they found. However, over the next 400 years, most Europeans did not appreciate African art. They did not understand the traditions of African art and expected it to be realistic, like Western art. Many Europeans found African art strange and frightening and condemned it as 'crude' and 'primitive'.

African art and Cubism

It was not until the 20th century that artists began to look at the forms and patterns of African art with new eyes. In 1907, the French artist and sculptor, André Derain, persuaded his friend Pablo Picasso to visit the *Musée d'Ethnographie* in Paris. Picasso's reaction to the masks and sculptures that he saw there was a mixture of admiration and fear. He admired the strong lines and forms of African art, but also found it strange and disturbing. Picasso spent many hours sketching African masks

The Spanish artist Pablo Picasso painted this important picture, *Les Demoiselles d'Avignon* in 1907, the year he was introduced to African art. Until then, Western artists had rarely portrayed the human form in such a stark, geometric and abstract way. This was the beginning of a new style, called Cubism, which drew its inspiration from African art.

50

and used these studies as the basis for a bold new style of painting and sculpture, known as Cubism. Like many forms of African art, Western Cubist paintings and sculptures use bold, geometric patterns and do not attempt to show the human form or face in a realistic way.

A powerful influence

After Picasso, many other 20th-century artists studied African art. Henri Matisse, Georges Braque, Amadeo Modigliani and Maurice Utrillo were all influenced by African artists, producing **geometric**, almost **abstract** figures and using bold lines and colours.

Sculptors such as Constantin Brancusi and Henry Moore created strong, stylized figures inspired by African carvings and masks. Fabric designers adapted the abstract patterns used in African textiles, and musicians adapted the sounds and rhythms of African music. Jazz, soul and blues all have their roots in the powerful rhythms and looseness of African music, while more recent types of music, such as rap and hip-hop, copy the rhythmic use of the human voice often found in African music.

Recently, some artists have followed the practice used by many African artists of including '**found objects**' in their art, while modern performance artists have created works of art that combine costume, singing, music and dancing, in imitation of a traditional African ceremony.

Understanding African art

Although Western artists have learnt a great deal from African art, many Africans feel that their art is not properly understood and that their sacred objects are not treated with enough respect. In many Western museums, African carvings and

This mask-like sculpture was made by the Romanian sculptor, Constantin Brancusi around 1913. With its simplified features and strong, geometric shapes it is clearly influenced by African masks and carvings.

masks are presented as if they were simply curiosities, without any explanation of the important part that they play in the religious life of a society. However, some museums today are working hard to change this attitude. They are providing more information on African works of art, so that people can appreciate the beliefs and traditions that lie behind them.

African ethnic groups

When Africa was divided up into countries by the colonial powers, they did not always follow the boundaries that already existed between the ethnic groups living there. As a result, today many countries are home to more than one ethnic group, and some ethnic groups spread across several countries. Here is a list of the ethnic groups discussed in this book, as well as the area of Africa where they live today.

Ethnic group	Location
Akan	Ghana and Cote d'Ivoire
Asante	West Africa
Azande	Central Africa
Bamileke	Cameroon
Berber	North Africa
Dinka	Sudan
Do	Côte d'Ivoire
Dogon	Mali
Fulani	West Africa
Ga	Ghana
Himba	Southern Africa
Ife	West Africa
Kikuyu	Kenya
Konson	Ethiopia
Kuba	Congo
Lele	Congo
Luba	Congo
Maasai	Kenya, Tanzania
Madi	Uganda, Sudan
Makonde	East Africa

Ethnic group	Location
Mangbetu	Central Africa
Mbuti	Congo River
Mende	Sierra Leone
Mossi	Burkina Faso
Ndebele	Southern Africa
Nuba	Sudan
Nuer	Sudan
Pygmy	Central African rainforest
San	Botswana, South Africa
Shona	Zimbabwe, Mozambique
Tuareg	Niger, Nigeria, Burkina Faso, Senegal, Mali
Tutsi	Rwanda, Burundi
Yoruba	Nigeria, Benin
Zande	Sudan/Congo borders
Zulu	Southern Africa

Further resources

More books to read

Ayo, Yvonne, *Eyewitness Guides: Africa* (Dorling Kindersley, 1995)

Golding, Vivien, *Traditions from Africa* (Wayland, 1998)

Mirow, Gregory, *Traditional African Designs* (Dover Design Library, 1997)

Websites

http://www.africanart.org/
The website of the Musuem for African Art, New York.

http://www.africancrafts.com/
The website of African crafts online. Provides profiles of a wide range of craftworkers from all over Africa and includes demonstrations of different craft techniques.

http://www.lam.mus.ca.us/africa/main.htm
An online catalogue for a travelling exhibition of African art, with activities for children.

http://www.nmafa.si.edu/
The website of the Smithsonian Museum, providing an illustrated guide to the collection.

http://www.webzinemaker.net/africans-art/index.php3?action=page&id_art=387
The website of the Nok Museum, a virtual museum of African Arts with many links to other sites.

Places to visit

UK

Pitt-Rivers Museum, Oxford

Sainsbury African Galleries, British Museum, London

USA

Art Institute of Chicago, Illinois

Bayly Art Museum, University of Virginia, Charlottesville, Virginia

Museum for African Art, Long Island City, Queens, New York

St Louis Art Museum, St Louis, Missouri

Smithsonian National Museum of African Art, Washington D.C.

Glossary

abstract showing an idea rather than a thing

AIDS serious illness in which the body's ability to protect itself against disease is destroyed. AIDS stands for acquired immune deficiency syndrome.

archaeologist someone who studies the past by digging up old buildings and objects and examining them carefully

bellows an instrument used for pumping air into a fire

Byzantines people who lived in the Byzantine Empire, which covered Greece, Turkey and parts of North Africa, and lasted from 395 CE to 1453

calabash a tall, long-necked gourd, that is dried and hollowed out and used as a container

civil war fighting between different groups of people within the same country

colony area or a country that is controlled by people from a different country

commission to pay someone to create something, such as a work of art

conical shaped like a cone

cut-pile raffia cloth that has patterns stitched into it

earplug flat, round earring covering and stretching the lower part of the ear

engraving shapes or letters cut into the surface of wood, metal or glass, using a sharp tool

ethnic group group of people who share the same ancestors, customs and laws

fibre fine thread

fire to bake a pot in a furnace until it is hard

found object item used by an artist that has been discovered, rather than being made by the artist

furnace very hot oven used to fire pots

geometric a design of regular, often repeated lines and shapes

glaze to cover a pot with a thin coat of liquid, that gives it a shiny finish

gourd fruit whose shell can be dried and used to make cups and musical instruments

idealize to make something look perfect

initiation ceremony to welcome young boys or girls to adult life

masquerade a masked dance

membrane thin layer, often made from skin

mosque building where Muslims pray

Muslim someone whose religion is based on the teachings of the Prophet Muhammad and on the holy book, the Qur'an

naturalistic looking very like the thing that it is meant to represent

nomad someone with no permanent home, who moves around from place to place

obelisk tall stone pillar with a square or rectangular base and sides that narrow to a point

ochre a colour made from soil and used for painting or dyeing

pendant item that hangs down from a fixed point

Persia an ancient Middle Eastern country that is now Iran

pharaoh ancient Egyptian king

pigment a substance that gives colour to something

puberty time when a boy or girl's body changes from a child's to an adult's

raffia fibres made from the leaves of the raffia palm

resonator box or case in a musical instrument that makes sounds louder and stronger

sahel scrub, drier than savannah

savannah dry, hot grassland

scarification the art of making patterns of scars on the body

shantytown area of homes lived in by very poor people, often made from cardboard or corrugated iron

shrine sacred building or place, where people worship or where something holy is kept

stylized bold and not realistic

terracotta orangey-red clay

textile a fabric or cloth

throwing-stick a curved stick, rather like a boomerang, used by desert hunters in South Africa to stun or kill their prey

tie-dye method of dyeing cloth in which parts of the cloth are tied tightly so they are not coloured by the dye

Vandals group of people who invaded parts of the Roman Empire around 400 CE

Index